Discovering

SQUIRRELS

Adrian Davies

The Bookwright Press
New York · 1987

Discovering Nature

Discovering Ants
Discovering Bees and Wasps
Discovering Beetles
Discovering Birds of Prey
Discovering Butterflies and Moths
Discovering Crickets and Grasshoppers
Discovering Flies

Discovering Frogs and Toads
Discovering Rabbits and Hares
Discovering Snakes and Lizards
Discovering Spiders
Discovering Squirrels
Discovering Worms

Further titles are in preparation

All photographs from Oxford Scientific Films

First published in the
United States in 1987 by
The Bookwright Press
387 Park Avenue South
New York, NY 10016

First published in 1986 by
Wayland (Publishers) Limited
61 Western Road, Hove
East Sussex BN3 1JD, England

© Copyright 1986 Wayland (Publishers) Limited

ISBN 0-531-18100-6
Library of Congress Catalog Card Number: 86-71273

Typeset by Alphabet Limited
Printed in Italy by Sagdos S.p.A., Milan

Cover *A red squirrel sitting in a pine tree.*

Frontispiece *A gray squirrel running along a clothesline.*

Contents

1
What are Squirrels?

A gray squirrel holding a nut in its front paws.

Introducing Squirrels

Squirrels are small, furry animals with bushy tails. They are common not only in the country, but also in many city parks and gardens, where they often become tame enough to be fed by hand. But not all squirrels are like this. In fact, there are over 260 different types of squirrels.

Many squirrels live in forests and spend all their time in the tree tops. Some squirrels can glide quite long distances from tree to tree. Other squirrels dig burrows and live underground, often in large **colonies** Squirrels can be found in forests, prairies, mountains and even some desert areas. The only parts of the world without squirrels are Australia and New Zealand, Madagascar, southern South America, the Polar regions and the hottest deserts.

Squirrels belong to a group of

taught to perform tricks at medieval fairs, and prairie dogs feature in the legends of the North American Indians.

bove *A rock squirrel of North America with piece of food in its paws.*

nimals called **rodents.** Other odents include beavers, rats, mice nd hamsters. All rodents have sharp, urved front teeth called **incisors**, vhich are used to gnaw or grind food.

Squirrels have had a long association vith humans. Red squirrels were kept s pets by the Romans, marmots were

Above *A black-tailed prairie dog, a kind of ground squirrel, peeking out of its burrow to make sure the coast is clear.*

What Squirrels Look Like

Squirrels have long bodies, with short or long, bushy tails. Most squirrels ha[ve] soft, fine hair. Those living in cold reg[ions] such as Siberia, have very thick fur. Some squirrels, such as the European red squirrel, have long tufts [of] hair on their ears. Many squirrels are brightly colored and some, such as the American 13-lined ground squirrel, ha[ve] stripes on their bodies.

Squirrels have large eyes and sharp eyesight. This is essential when they are leaping from tree to tree in the forest. Some squirrels can see in color, something that most other **mammals** cannot do. Squirrels also have very good hearing and a well developed sense of touch through their touch-sensitive whiskers called vibrissae.

The European red squirrel has long tufts of hair on its ears.

These whiskers are found on the head, feet and legs.

Squirrels have long, powerful back legs on which they sit when feeding. Their shorter front legs are strong, and equipped with sharp claws. Burrowing ground squirrels use their long claws for digging. Tree squirrels use their claws to help them cling to tree trunks. Desert-living squirrels have hair on the soles of their feet, which forms a protective barrier against the hot sand.

Like all rodents, squirrels have two pairs of chisel-shaped incisor teeth. These continue to grow throughout the squirrel's life. To keep them from getting too long the squirrel gnaws hard objects such as wood and nuts.

This is a gray squirrel. Like other types of squirrels, it sits on its strong back legs when feeding.

The Squirrel's Tail

Most squirrels have long bushy tails. The tail is often held over the back while sitting or feeding. The name squirrel comes from two Greek words meaning "shade tail." The Kalahari ground squirrel lives in the hot, dry

A striped ground squirrel from Africa digging a hole. It fluffs its tail over its back to provide shade from the hot sun.

Kalahari Desert where there is very little natural shade. The squirrel fluffs out its tail and holds it like a parasol over its back, to provide shade from the intense heat of the sun.

Most squirrels that live in trees have longer tails than those living in burrows under the ground. Tree squirrels' tails are usually at least as long as the rest of their bodies. Tree squirrels are very agile and leap from tree to tree in their search for food. Their long tails act like rudders, guiding them through the air. Flying squirrels make up a group of remarkable tree squirrels. They glide through the air using their tails to steer themselves. The tails of flying squirrels are slightly flattened, which helps increase the steering effect.

The bushy tail is very useful for helping to keep warm at night, and squirrels wrap it around them when they sleep, rather like a blanket.

A young gray squirrel eating a piece of apple. Squirrels often hold their tails over their backs when sitting or feeding.

Ground squirrels use their tails to communicate signals to each other, warning of potential danger.

Because the squirrel's tail is so important, the squirrel spends much time grooming it, so the fine hairs do not stick together with dirt.

2
Different Kinds of Squirrels

A red squirrel uses its sharp claws to grip the bark as it climbs up a pine tree.

Tree Squirrels

Animals that live in trees are known as **arboreal**, and there are many kinds of arboreal squirrels. These include the familiar red and gray squirrels found in most forests of the world. Tree squirrels spend most of their time in the tree tops, but many do come down to the ground to look for fallen nuts and other food.

Tree squirrels are very agile, running along tree branches, and jumping from tree to tree. When on the ground they move in a series of graceful leaps, often stopping to look and listen for possible danger.

Most tree squirrels are fairly quiet animals, though if threatened, many squirrels will make a chattering noise. Many tree squirrels, and some ground squirrels, too, **molt** twice a year, in spring and autumn. Usually the summer coat is a lighter color than the

Left *Tree squirrels do not hibernate but they do sleep for several days at a time if the weather is very severe.*

winter coat, which is thicker to provide more warmth.

Tree squirrels do not **hibernate**, but they do become less active in winter. They are vulnerable to cold and damp, and may huddle together for warmth. In extremely cold weather, they may stay in their nests for several days at a time, only coming out to find food.

All tree squirrels are active during the day, especially in the early morning and in the late afternoon when they gather food before darkness falls.

Above *Tree squirrels, like this gray one, always descend trees head first.*

Flying Squirrels

A few kinds of tree squirrels do not just jump from tree to tree, they glide. This is not really true flight because the squirrels do not have wings. Instead, the flying squirrels have a large, furry membrane called a **patagium**, which extends from the front legs to the back legs. When the squirrel launches itself from a tree it extends its legs and the patagium acts rather like a parachute, helping the squirrel to glide through the air. By using the tail as a rudder, and varying the angle of the patagium, the squirrel can steer through the trees, and possibly avoid **predators**.

As the squirrel comes in to land, it brakes by turning its tail and body upward, and extending its legs. It lands flat against the tree trunk, its

A flying squirrel outside its nest in a hollow of the tree you can see above its head.

Three southern flying squirrels of North America: 1. The squirrel's gliding flight; 2. Coming in to land; 3. Feeding.

claws helping it to grip the bark.

Gliding is an economical way to travel, as it uses up very little energy. The cat-sized giant flying squirrels of the tropics can glide distances of well over 100 m (328 ft), but most of the smaller types can manage only short distances.

The patagium is fairly bulky and when folded away it does reduce the squirrel's mobility a little. It is probably for this reason that flying squirrels are nocturnal, that is, they are active only at night. They spend the day in the nest, which is usually in a hole in a hollow tree trunk.

A woman feeding chipmunks in a park.

Ground Squirrels

Animals that live on the ground are called **terrestrial** animals, and there are several different kinds of terrestrial squirrels. These include marmots, prairie dogs, chipmunks and sousliks. Some of these, particularly the marmots, can grow as big as a cat. Most are well built animals with short legs and are far less agile than tree squirrels. Marmots and prairie dogs have shorter, less bushy tails than tree squirrels.

There is one ground squirrel that is very agile. It is the chipmunk, a well-known visitor to campsites and picnic areas in North America. It is a great acrobat and can even turn somersaults.

Most terrestrial squirrels dig burrows in the ground in which to live. These are dug with the powerful front legs and can, in some cases, be very long. The American 13-lined ground squirrel sometimes digs

urrows up to 60 m (200 ft) long.
'nlike tree squirrels, ground squirrels
ften live together in large **colonies**.

In common with most other
quirrels, ground squirrels are mainly
egetarian, eating seeds, nuts, fruit,
erries and vegetables.

Ground-living squirrels are active

Young black-tailed prairie dogs at the entrance to their burrow. They stay close to home in case of danger.

during the day, especially in the morning and late afternoon. Many of them sleep, or hibernate, for long periods during the winter.

3
Where Squirrels Live

Many kinds of ground squirrels live in places like this, the desert of Monument Valley in Arizona.

Squirrels Around the World

Because squirrels eat a wide variety o plant food, they can live in most of the **habitats** where plants are found. They live in forests all over the world from tropical rainforests to much colder forests in Russia. They live on rocky cliffs and mountains, in desert and prairies and in city parks and gardens.

As we have seen, squirrels tend to be either terrestrial or arboreal. Arboreal squirrels either live in holes in tree trunks, often taking over abandoned woodpecker holes, or they build nests called **dreys**. Dreys are usually ball-shaped, and are made of twigs, leaves and other plant material. Often, squirrels will have a summer and a winter drey. The winter drey is usually built in the fork between the main trunk of the tree and a branch, while the summer drey is often built out on a

*bove Many tree squirrels live in coniferous
forests where there is plenty of food for them
to store for winter.*

ranch away from the trunk. One
quirrel may build several dreys. The
inside is usually lined with grass,
moss or other soft material.

Most terrestrial squirrels dig
urrows in open ground, though some
marmots, living in mountainous
egions, dig burrows underneath
ocks and boulders. Chipmunks, too,
ve in burrows under logs and rocks.

*A gray squirrel's winter drey built in the fork
of an oak tree.*

Towns and Cities

In many parts of the world, and particularly in North America and Europe, squirrels live in the parks and gardens of towns and cities.

Squirrels find plenty to eat in town parks and gardens where there are lots of trees and other plants. Squirrels get food from other sources too. They are often seen raiding garbage cans looking for scraps left over from somebody's lunch. Squirrel

A gray squirrel taking nuts put out for the birds.

an become very tame in parks and ardens, and will let people feed them y hand.

In general, squirrels do no harm in ur towns, and most people welcome hem as an attractive addition to rban wildlife. Occasionally, owever, squirrels damage trees by ripping the bark from them, or they ay eat baby birds. They are quick to ike advantage of the food which any people put out for birds. They ave even been seen moving, like ghtrope walkers, along clotheslines get at bags of nuts or seeds put out r birds.

Most squirrels that live in towns nd cities are tree squirrels, although the United States chipmunks e common in parks and gardens.

In cold countries squirrels metimes shelter in bird houses. As any as nine gray squirrels have been und in one bird house, huddled

Some squirrels are tame enough to be fed by hand. This gray squirrel is enjoying being fed nuts.

together, their tails fluffed out to keep in the warmth. Squirrels have also been found nesting in the roofs of houses, using the roof insulation material to build their nests.

Prairie-dog "Towns"

A black-tailed prairie-dog town. These "towns" can cover large areas of land.

Prairie dogs are small ground-living squirrels, found in the open plains, or prairies, of North America. They are **social** animals and live together in family groups called **coteries**. Each coterie may have five adults and

When black-tailed prairie dogs meet they touch noses as a form of greeting.

several young. There will usually be many coteries in an area, their boundaries joining each other to form a "town." These towns can be huge — some have been known to cover an area as large as 160 acres, containing thousands of prairie dogs.

All the animals from a coterie use all parts of the burrow system. When members of a coterie meet each other they often touch noses. This serves not only as a greeting but also helps them to recognize each other.

Each coterie has its own boundary, which, during autumn and winter, is defended by the dominant male. He will bark at, and chase off, intruders from other coteries. During the summer the boundaries are relaxed and friendly contacts with neighboring coteries are common.

A **breeding** coterie usually consists of one male and four females. When the prairie dogs are born, both males and females help care for them. Non-breeding coteries may have several males and females. One male usually dominates the rest.

When the burrows become overcrowded, some adult prairie dogs leave to dig new burrows at the edge of the town. This is good for the colony as the more experienced animals colonize new territory, while the younger animals are left in safer, familiar surroundings.

4
Food and Feeding

A red squirrel reaches up to get some blackberries to eat.

What Squirrels Eat

Most squirrels eat nuts, seeds, fruit, leaves, grass and other plant material. When this kind of food cannot be found squirrels will eat insects, birds' eggs and even baby birds.

Some squirrels, for example the long-nosed squirrels of Malaysia, eat ants, termites and other insects. These squirrels have very long, slender lower incisors, and short upper ones. They are used like a pair of tweezers to pick up the small insects.

When squirrels feed they sit upright on their haunches, holding the food in their front paws. The food is turned between the paws as it is being eaten.

Hard-shelled nuts are eaten by gnawing a small hole in the shell, and then using the teeth to pry the nut apart. In those parts of the world where coconuts are found, there are

These chewed remains of pine cones show that squirrels have been feeding here.

squirrels that can break through the very hard shell to eat the soft coconut inside.

Above *A gray squirrel about to eat an apple.*

Pine cones are an important food for many squirrels. The squirrel holds the base of the cone in its paws and pulls out the winged seeds. Each tiny seed is extracted and the wing blows away. Squirrels drink very little, obtaining all the water they need from their food, or the dew on the food.

Hoarding Food

Squirrels are well known as hoarders of food. This is because food is not always available all year round. So some squirrels hide nuts, seeds and other food to be eaten at a later date. They dig holes in the ground, drop the food in, and then cover it up with soil and leaves.

Squirrels do not remember where they bury food. Instead they search an area and find the food using their

A gray squirrel collecting acorns to be eaten in the winter months when food is scarce.

acute sense of smell. A red squirrel can locate a pine cone buried 30 cm (12 in) under the ground. Squirrels do not always find the food they have buried, but they may well find another squirrel's hidden stores.

The buried nuts and seeds that are not found may well **germinate** and grow into new plants. In this way squirrels help the spread of many trees in the forest. Gray squirrels have been known to carry acorns from oak trees over 30 m (100 ft) from where they were found. In North America the Douglas pine squirrel helps the spread of **coniferous** trees, hiding stores of up to 160 cones under logs or in hollow stumps.

Chipmunks sleep for long periods in the winter and store food in their burrows. They carry this food in large cheek pouches. The food is eaten when the chipmunk wakes during the winter.

A gray squirrel burying food. Squirrels do not always remember where they store food. They use their acute sense of smell to find it.

5
The Life History of Squirrels

These North American red squirrels are only a few days old.

Reproduction

In order to reproduce, male and female squirrels need to join together, or **mate**. During mating, the male squirrel injects his **sperm** into the female's body, to fertilize her eggs.

Most squirrels mate during or immediately after winter, and produce their young from three to six weeks later. Some squirrels have two breeding seasons, one in spring and, if the weather is good, another in summer.

Before mating, several male tree squirrels will often chase one female, but only one will mate with her. After mating, the males play no further part in the rearing of the young. On the other hand, both male and female marmots, and other ground squirrels, tend the young.

The female tree squirrel gives birth to between one and six young in her

aby red squirrels in their nest. Their eyes ave not yet opened.

When they are about four weeks old, baby red squirrels begin to explore outside their nest.

drey. When they are born, the young squirrels are blind, hairless and helpless. They grow quickly, and by the age of three weeks they will have grown fur. They open their eyes at about four weeks. They become increasingly mobile, leaving the nest or the first time at about seven

weeks. They start to take solid food at this time and will be fully **weaned** from their mother by about eight weeks. The young squirrels will stay close to their mother until they get used to their surroundings. Most squirrels are able to breed when they are one year old.

Hibernation and Aestivation

Terrestrial squirrels, living in regions where winters are severe, hibernate for many months of the year. Hibernation is a remarkable process. All the body functions slow down, the body temperature drops dramatically to just above the freezing point and the heartbeat and breathing rate slow

A golden-mantled squirrel gathering bedding for its hibernation nest in Yellowstone National Park.

down, so that the animal seems quite lifeless.

Before hibernating the squirrel eats lots of food and grows fat. This fat supplies the body during the winter with the necessary energy to keep the body processes going. A marmot, weighing 4½ kg (10 lb) at the start of hibernation, may weigh only half this when it wakes up. By going into this state of "suspended animation" squirrels are able to survive long cold winters without food.

In the coldest regions, marmots may hibernate for eight or nine months. The entire family of up to fifteen animals retreats into the burrow and huddles together. The last animal into the burrow usually closes the entrance with some grass or earth.

One type of American marmot, the woodchuck or ground hog, is traditionally believed to emerge from hibernation on February 2, which is called "ground-hog day."

Some squirrels, such as the little souslik, hibernate not only in winter, but also during the hottest, driest parts of the summer, when all the plants have withered from the lack of rain. This summer sleeping is called aestivation. It is very similar to hibernation.

A golden-mantled ground squirrel hibernating. It will sleep in its nest throughout the winter.

6
Survival in a Dangerous World

A golden eagle eating a ground squirrel.

Enemies of Squirrels

Because squirrels are usually alert and agile, they have relatively few natural predators, although they are caught and eaten by a number of different animals and birds. Squirrels are eaten by weasels, foxes, coyotes, bobcats and badgers. Eagles, hawks and owls will also catch squirrels for food. Prairie dogs are often caught by rattle-snakes. It is usually the weaker or older squirrels and the young, inexperienced squirrels that are caught. In towns and cities, cats and dogs catch squirrels, but more are killed by cars.

Probably the greatest threat to squirrels comes from humans. Through the ages we have caught squirrels for their meat and for their fur. In cold countries squirrel fur is soft and thick in winter, and large numbers are caught each year for

A man putting down a cage trap in the forest to catch squirrels.

Cutting down forests destroys the tree squirrel's natural habitat.

their **pelts**. Squirrel tails are also used to make paint brushes.

Another way in which humans kill squirrels is by destroying their habitat. Each year vast areas of forest, particularly tropical rainforest, are destroyed to make way for agriculture.

The squirrels living there cannot live anywhere else, and so, if too much of their habitat is destroyed, they will die out. In much the same way, destruction of the prairie dogs' natural habitat has greatly reduced their numbers.

The Cautious Squirrel

Because squirrels are eaten by a variety of predators, they are naturally cautious. When looking for food on the forest floor, squirrels often stop to listen and look for signs of danger. They are also alert when feeding, and

This golden-mantled squirrel of North America is very alert and ready to run if it senses danger.

ready to run at the slightest sound. When on the ground, tree squirrels rarely stray far from a tree up which they can flee. Although squirrels take over rapidly, they soon peep out from their hiding places to see if the danger has passed.

Tree squirrels can not only jump from tree to tree, but also run up and down tree trunks with ease. They use their long claws to grip the bark. Squirrels always come down a tree head first, and often wait, holding onto the trunk a little way above the ground, for some moments before finally descending.

A female squirrel with young in the nest is extra careful because many predators may take her babies. She will not hesitate to move them if danger threatens, carrying them in her mouth. Adult social terrestrial squirrels, such as the marmots, usually stand guard while the young play and feed. A complex series of calls is used to warn of danger. Marmots whistle, and prairie dogs bark.

A black-tailed prairie dog calls to warn others that danger is nearby.

7
Squirrels as Pests

The gray squirrel causes extensive damage to trees by eating buds and shoots, thereby destroying the tree's new growth.

Squirrels and Humans

Squirrels are pests to farmers because they eat grass, vegetables and other plants. The many thousands of animals in a large prairie dog town can eat a tremendous amount of food. They damage more than they eat, ruining large areas of crops. Squirrels may also damage orchards and fruit crops, eating young buds and shoots as well as the fruit itself.

An animal may become a pest if it is introduced by humans into areas where it has very few predators and an abundant food source. Gray squirrels were introduced into Britain in the early 20th century, from North America. They quickly spread, and today are found in most parts of Britain. At the same time, the population of the native red squirrel began to decline. It was thought that the gray squirrels were causing this,

This nest box, put out for the birds, has been damaged by gray squirrels.

possibly even fighting the reds and killing them, but it is now known that the red squirrel was suffering from a disease. In many areas the gray squirrel moved into the red squirrel's territory.

Red squirrels are again on the increase, but it seems unlikely that they will be able to move back into areas now occupied by the gray. An attempt is currently being made in Britain to reintroduce the red squirrel into certain areas. They have been released into Regent's Park, in London, and a check will be kept on how they fare alongside the gray squirrel.

Red squirrels are far less common in Britain than their more numerous relative the gray squirrel.

Bark-stripping

Several kinds of squirrels strip bark, although the gray squirrel is the worst offender, earning itself the nickname "tree-rat" in some places.

The squirrel gnaws away at a section of bark until it makes a hole. It then pulls off the bark in strips. It strips bark either from the trunk of the tree if the bark is not too thick, or from the branches. Precisely why squirrels strip bark is still not known. It is thought that they like eating the sweet, sappy tissue found immediately underneath the bark.

Trees can survive a certain amount of bark stripping, but if the bark is removed in a complete ring around the trunk or branch, then the damage is much more serious. If the trunk is

A gray squirrel feeding on the bark of a sycamore tree.

ring-barked" then the whole tree will die. If one of the branches is ring-barked then all of the branch above that point will die, possibly causing the branch to snap off.

Even with only a small amount of bark stripping, a tree is more open to disease and attack from **fungi** and

The tree on which this red squirrel is feeding will probably die because so much of its bark has been stripped.

insects. If the tree is being grown to be sold, perhaps for the furniture industry, then its value will be greatly reduced.

8
Studying Squirrels

A gray squirrel eating peanuts in Regent's Park, London.

It is quite easy to watch gray squirrels in the wild. If you live in a town or a city you will be able to see them in your local park. Squirrels also visit people's gardens for food. Some squirrels are quite tame and will take food from your hand.

If you live in the country you may be able to see tree squirrels in areas of woodland. Ground squirrels are more likely to be seen in areas of grassland, though a few kinds may live in urban areas. Flying squirrels are not easy to see because they are active mainly at night.

You can tempt squirrels out of the trees, or from their burrows, by putting out food for them. Some of the things they like to eat are nuts, seeds and fruit. If you regularly put out food in the same place you may eventually get a whole family of squirrels coming out to feed.

Squirrels are easily scared away –

If you are lucky you may see a squirrel collecting nesting material, which is what this round-tailed ground squirrel of California is doing.

This gray squirrel has learned to come to the windowsill for food.

The slightest noise or fast movement will send them running back to the safety of their nest. But they will soon come out to eat again if you are quiet and patient.

Glossary

Arboreal Living in trees.
Breeding Producing and rearing young.
Colonies Groups of the same type of animal or plant living together.
Coniferous Trees that stay green all year round and have cones and needle-shaped leaves, such as pine and fir trees.
Coteries Family groups of prairie dogs.
Dreys Squirrels' nests.
Fungi Plants without green coloration, such as mushrooms and molds.
Germinate To begin to sprout and grow.
Habitats The natural homes of animals and
plants.
Hibernate To sleep for weeks or months during the winter.
Incisors Long, front teeth with sharp, chisel-shaped edges used for gnawing.
Mammals A group of warm-blooded animals with backbones. The females have glands that produce milk to feed their young.

Mate The way in which male and female animals join so that the female's eggs are fertilized by the male's sperm.
Molt To shed an old coat of fur gradually and grow a new one in its place.
Patagium The furry membrane between the front and back legs which, when extended, helps the flying squirrel to glide.
Pelts The skins of furry animals, used to make fur coats.
Predators Animals that kill other animals for food.
Rodents A group of animals having one pair of incisors in each jaw, and no canine teeth.
Social Living together in a colony.
Sperm The male sex cells, which fertilize a female's eggs.
Terrestrial Living on land.
Urban Living in a city or a town.
Vegetarian An animal that eats plants.
Weaned No longer dependent on mother's milk.

Finding Out More

The following books will tell you more about squirrels:

Bernard, George and Paling, John. *The Grey Squirrel.* New York: Putnam Publishing Group, 1982.

Graham, Ada and Frank. *We Watch Squirrels.* New York: Dodd, Mead, 1985.
Lane, Margaret. *The Squirrel.* New York: Dial Books for Young Readers, 1981.
McConoughey, Jana. *The Squirrels.* Mankato, MN: Crestwood House, 1983.
Sabin, Frencene. *Mammals.* Mahwah, NJ: Troll Associates, 1985.

Index

Picture Ackowledgments

The photographs in this book were supplied by: Bruce Coleman Ltd: J. & D. Bartlett 16, E. & P. Bauer 25, N.G. Blake 13, R. Borland 12, J.M. Burley 37, E. Crichton 42, M.P.L. Fogden 32, J. Foott 19, 21 (left), 33, D. Goulston 11, L.B. Grande 31 (left), K. Gunnar 18, W. Laninen 30, C. Ott *cover*, H. Reinhard 10, L.L. Rue 9 (right), 15 (right), 24, 31 (right), 34, 41, J. Van Wormer 43 (right), F. Vollmar 35 (right), Adrian Davies 21 (right), 27 (left); GeoScience Features: Dr. B. Booth 9 (left), 20 G. Hirons 8, R. Macey 36, G. Webb 14, 39 (bottom); Oxford Scientific Films: G.I. Bernard 14 (left), 27 (right), 28, 29, J. Paling *Frontispiece*, 22, 35 (right), 38, 40, C.M. Perrins 39 (top), D.J. Saunders 26; A.J.R. Walters 23; Wayland Picture Library: Sarah McKenzie 43 (left). Artwork by Wendy Meadway.